Charlotte Guillain

Raintree is an imprint of Capstone Global Library Limited, a company incorporated in England and Wales having its registered office at 7 Pilgrim Street, London, EC4V 6LB – Registered company number: 6695582

www.raintreepublishers.co.uk
myorders@raintreepublishers.co.uk

Edited by Laura Knowles, Abby Colich, and Diyan Leake
Designed by Victoria Allen and Ken Vail Graphic Design
Original illustrations © Capstone Global Library Ltd 2013
Illustrated by HL Studios
Picture research by Elizabeth Alexander
Originated by Capstone Global Library Ltd
Printed and bound in China by CTPS

ISBN 978 1 406 25908 7 (hardback)
17 16 15 14 13
10 9 8 7 6 5 4 3 2 1

ISBN 978 1 406 25915 5 (paperback)
18 17 16 15 14
10 9 8 7 6 5 4 3 2 1

British Library Cataloguing in Publication Data
Guillain, Charlotte.
  Bats. -- (Animal abilities)
  1. Bats--Juvenile literature. 2. Animal intelligence--
  Juvenile literature.
  I. Title II. Series
  599.4-dc23

Acknowledgements
We would like to thank the following for permission to reproduce photographs: Alamy pp. 6 (© Wildscotphotos), 7 (© SuperStock/Barry Mansell), 10 (© blickwinkel), 11 (© SuperStock), 15 (© Ivan Kuzmin), 20 (© Scenics & Science), 22 (© Malcolm Schuyl), 23 (© Arterra Picture Library), 26 (© Chris Howes/Wild Places Photography), 29 (© Clownfishphoto); Nature Picture Library p. 16 (Barry Mansell); Science Photo Library p. 5 (Merlin Tuttle); Shutterstock pp. 4 (© Erik Zandboer), 12 (© Meaning), 18 (© Erkki & Hanna), 19 (© Ivan Kuzmin), 24 (© Monkey Business Images), 28 (© Ivan Kuzmin); (Superstock pp. 8 (© Minden Pictures), 13 (© Minden Pictures), 17 (© Minden Pictures), 21 (© imagebroker.net), 27 (© Minden Pictures). Design feature of a bat silhouette reproduced with permission of Shutterstock (© Vule).

Cover photograph of a grey long-eared bat reproduced with permission of Shutterstock (© Eric Isselée).

Every effort has been made to contact copyright holders of material reproduced in this book. Any omissions will be rectified in subsequent printings if notice is given to the publisher.

Contents

Some words are shown in bold, **like this**. You can find out what they mean by looking in the glossary.

Meet the bats

What do you think of when someone mentions bats? Do you think of vampires and darkness? Many people are scared of bats, or think they are creepy. But really bats are incredible!

Bats are the only **mammals** that have wings and can fly properly, rather than just glide. Bats make up one-fifth of all mammal **species** in the world. The only places in the world where they don't live are the Antarctic, near the North Pole, the most extreme deserts, and some remote islands. They can survive in many different **habitats**.

The kalong flying fox is the largest type of bat.

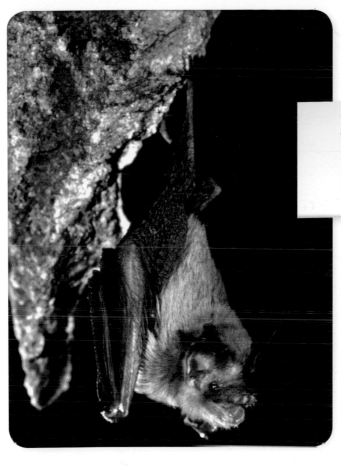

The bumblebee bat is the smallest bat in the world.

Rather than being dangerous to people, bats usually keep away from us. In many ways they help humans, by eating the insects that spread diseases and helping the plants we eat to grow. Bats also have amazing skills and abilities that make them stand out from many other animals.

HOW MANY?

There are more than 1,100 species of bat around the world.

Being a bat

Like all mammals, bats have hair on their bodies, are warm-blooded, and feed their babies with milk made by the mother. Like birds, they can use their wings to fly in search of food. Although bats live in a range of habitats, many species live in rainforests.

The fruit bats roost in trees.

Most bats are nocturnal, which means they move around during the night and rest during the day. Bats like to find safe, quiet places to hide and **roost** in the daytime, such as caves and the tops of trees. Most bats live in large groups called **colonies**, although some species live alone.

Groups of bats

There are two different groups of bats: **microbats** and **megabats**. Microbats live in most parts of the world. They have small eyes and mostly eat insects, although some eat plants, fish, frogs, or even blood! Megabats mainly live in the tropical rainforests of Africa and Asia, with some found in Australasia, and some islands in the South Pacific and Indian Ocean. They have large eyes and eat fruit and flowers.

Ghost-faced bats are microbats that roost in caves.

BIG EATERS

Even a small bat, such as the pipistrelle, can eat as many as 3,000 insects in one night!

Bat flight

Bats are **adapted** to fly because moving through the air helps them to reach the food that they eat. Whether they are chasing insects through the evening air or searching for fruit in high treetops, bats use their flying ability to feed.

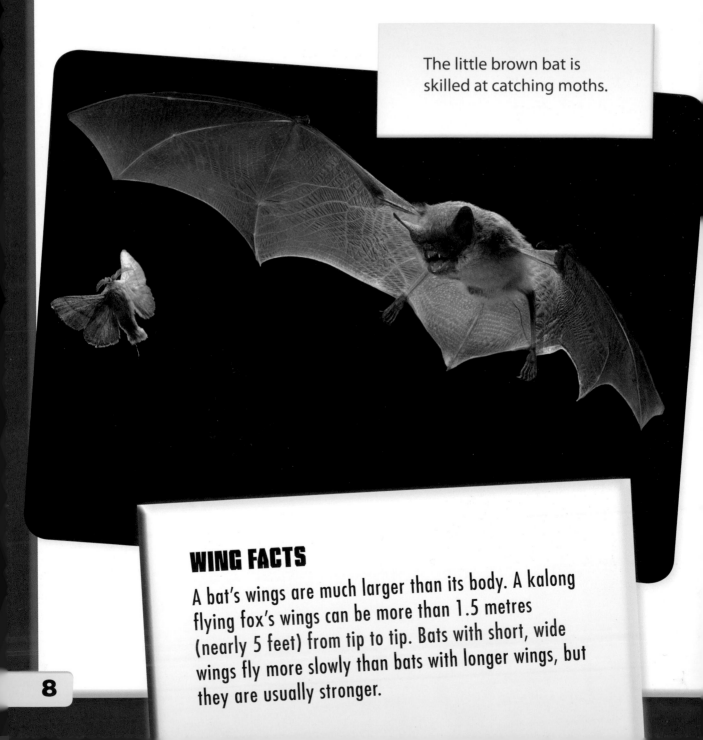

The little brown bat is skilled at catching moths.

WING FACTS

A bat's wings are much larger than its body. A kalong flying fox's wings can be more than 1.5 metres (nearly 5 feet) from tip to tip. Bats with short, wide wings fly more slowly than bats with longer wings, but they are usually stronger.

How bats' wings work

Bats flap their wings to fly, in a similar way to birds. But instead of feathers, a bat's wings have thin skin stretched from the arm bones to the bat's body and legs. Most of the bat's long fingers are part of the wing, but one thumb with a claw sticks out. Bats use this to help them walk, climb, or hold food.

Bats use a great deal of energy when they fly and this produces a lot of heat. But this heat can leave the bat's wings very quickly and this stops them from overheating.

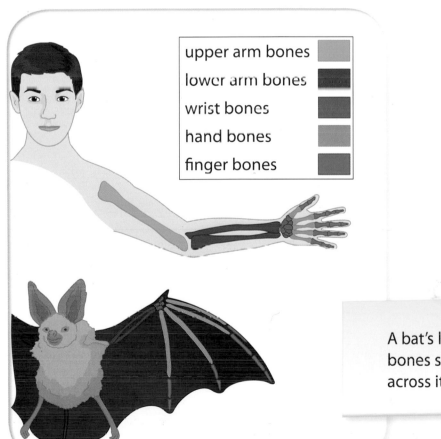

upper arm bones

lower arm bones

wrist bones

hand bones

finger bones

A bat's long finger bones stretch across its wings.

How bats fly

Bats' wings are very flexible. A bat can quickly turn each wing to change direction, and it can completely fold its wings up or stretch them out tightly. This flexibility helps bats when they fly into narrow spaces, such as caves, because they can fold up their wings as they come in to land.

This grey long-eared bat can fold its wings to fit through a small space.

The fastest bats can fly at more than 48 kilometres (30 miles) per hour. Many bats are also able to **hover** while they are feeding.

The lesser long-nosed bat can hover as it feeds on nectar from plants.

HOW DO WE KNOW?

Scientists are investigating how bats control their flight. Research has shown that tiny hairs on bats' wings might work as airflow sensors, telling the bats when they need to adjust their movements. Scientists built an **artificial** forest for bats to fly through in the dark. Then they removed the hairs from the bats' wings. Without the hairs, the bats' flight was slower and less precise. They also had less control over their balance while they were flying.

Hanging out

Bats are most agile when they fly. Their legs are weak and most bats struggle to walk on the ground. Bats' legs are also too weak to push off with when they begin to fly. But bats have adapted to hang upside down or sideways when they roost, or to perch in very high places. This means that when they want to take off and fly, they can just fall from their perch and start flying.

Hanging upside down high up in caves also helps to keep bats out of the way of **predators**, such as birds of prey. Hanging up high in large groups in trees also provides safety in numbers.

These bats can hang upside down on a rock wall.

Getting a grip

A bat has specially adapted feet to help it to roost upside down. The feet automatically grip onto a surface without the bat having to think about holding on. This means the bat can sleep while hanging upside down, with its feet firmly gripping onto its perch.

ENERGY SAVERS

Some bats are able to lower their own body temperature when they roost. This helps them to save energy while they rest, so they have more energy when they need to fly.

Leaf-nosed bats grip on to tree branches as they roost.

Bat senses

Most microbats hunt for moving **prey**, such as insects, as they fly around in the dark. Their sight is about as strong as a human's, but this is not enough to locate their prey at night. They have to use **echolocation**.

Bats make very high squeaking noises as they fly, and they use the echo that comes back to sense what is around them and how far away it is. They can change the pitch of their squeaks to tell the difference between obstacles and prey, so they can avoid hitting trees or buildings while still catching their prey.

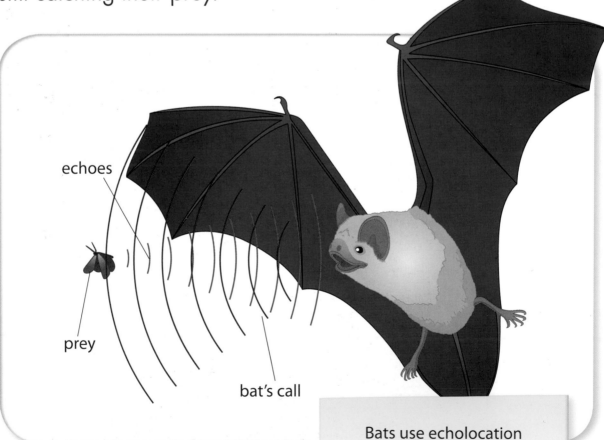

echoes

prey

bat's call

Bats use echolocation to find small, moving prey in the dark.

Whispering bats

Barbastelle bats hunt moths that can pick up the bats' high-pitched squeaks and escape. But the bats have adapted to this by learning to whisper their echolocation calls! This means the bats can get up close to the moths and **ambush** them.

Scientists think bats' large ears help them detect the echoes in echolocation.

HOW DO WE KNOW?

Scientists discovered how bats sneak up on their prey by observing moths' ears as they listened to different bats' echolocation. The whispering barbastelle could get very close to the moth before it could be heard.

Sensing heat and smell

Vampire bats feed on the blood of other animals. They bite into an animal's skin and then drink the blood. Vampire bats use echolocation, sight, and smell to find their prey.

Vampire bats have another special sense that helps them feed. In a vampire bat's nose, there are sensors called thermoreceptors, which can sense heat or cold. The thermoreceptors tell the bat where blood is close to the surface of their prey's skin, so they know where to bite.

A vampire bat is drinking blood from this chicken's foot.

Megabat senses

Most megabats don't use echolocation to find their food. They have much larger eyes and a stronger sense of sight than microbats, and so use their eyes to spot fruits and flowers. Megabats can see much better than humans in the dark. They also use their very strong sense of smell to find flowers full of ripe fruits and nectar.

The spectacled flying fox's large eyes help it to find food.

CLICKING BAT

The Egyptian fruitbat is one of a few megabats to use echolocation. It makes high-pitched clicks inside the dark caves where it roosts. The echoes tell the bats where the rock face is so that they can avoid hitting it as they fly.

Colonies and communication

Many species of bat live in **colonies**. There may be millions of bats in one microbat colony in a large cave. Flying foxes can form colonies in trees made up of hundreds of thousands of bats.

These flying foxes can be seen roosting in treetops during the day.

Why live in a colony?

Many bats live together in colonies to share each other's warmth as they roost, especially during cold winter months. Living together in large numbers also helps to keep bats safe. Some bats in a colony will even bring food back for other members of their group who are too ill to hunt.

This colony of lesser mouse-eared bats is roosting close together upside down in a cave.

Talking bats?

Although their calls are too high pitched for humans to hear properly, bats communicate with other members of their colony. Male bats have their own special call when they want to attract a female. Bats also call to mark out their **territory**, scare away other animals, teach their young, and recognize other bats in their colony.

HOW DO WE KNOW?

Scientists use special detectors to record bats making many different sounds to each other within a colony.

Caring and sharing

When female bats are pregnant, they often gather together in groups. They give birth to their babies and then stay together as they care for their young. Most bats only give birth to one baby, called a pup, but some species may have up to four babies.

BIGGEST COLONY

The largest bat colony in the world comes together every summer in a cave in Texas, USA. Around 20 million bats join the colony, and the females give birth to their young there.

This colony of fruit bats is roosting in a cave in Malaysia.

The pups hold on to their roosting mothers with their back legs. Most baby bats feed on their mother's milk for about six weeks. It's usually at least two months before young bats start to fly.

Some species of microbat help each other when the females are caring for their young. A mother bat can leave her baby with another female so that she can go out to hunt. When she comes back, she can find her pup by listening for its sounds and smelling it. Not many animals help each other in this way.

This fruit bat pup is clinging on to its mother as she roosts.

BAT FRIENDS

Some bats form smaller, special groups within a colony. The bats in these smaller groups can have close relationships over long periods of time.

Surviving winter

Some bats travel to other places to avoid winter or move to a warmer climate where there are more insects. This movement is called migration.

HOW DO WE KNOW?

Bats use a lot of energy when they migrate, so it's important that they don't get lost. Scientists have discovered that bats have a **magnetic** substance in their bodies, which they use to help them find their way. Researchers did experiments using powerful magnets and discovered that magnetite in the bats' bodies works with Earth's magnetic field to tell them which direction to fly.

As well as navigating using Earth's magnetic field, bats use sight, the position of the Sun, and echolocation to find their way.

Many species of bat migrate to the same spot each year, with individual bats even roosting in the same place each time. Some species of bat do not migrate far, while others, such as the little brown bat, can travel as far as 800 kilometres (500 miles).

Hibernation

Some bats **hibernate** during winter. This means they sleep to save energy while temperatures are cold, living on stores of body fat. During hibernation, a bat's heart only beats about 11 times a minute. When a bat flies, its heart beats over 1,000 times a minute.

These whiskered bats are hibernating in a cellar.

Copying bats

Humans are very interested in bats and their special skills. Scientists have used technology to mimic the way bats use echoes to map their surroundings.

Ultrasound

Ultrasound is used by doctors to make images of the insides of people's bodies. An ultrasound machine sends out high-pitched sounds when it is placed on someone's body, and the echoes that come back are used to make a picture of what's inside. This can help to find problems when a patient is ill.

Ultrasound is used to check on babies developing inside pregnant women.

Robots

Researchers are exploring the ways echolocation can be used by robotic vehicles. These vehicles go to places that are too small or dangerous for humans to enter to find information. They can use ultrasound to find their way over difficult ground or to spot damage.

BAT SENSES

Some people who have difficulty seeing have learned to use a form of echolocation to find their way around. They make clicking noises and listen to the echoes the sounds make to work out if anything is in their path.

People use a system of underwater echolocation called sonar to measure distances and spot submarines and schools of fish.

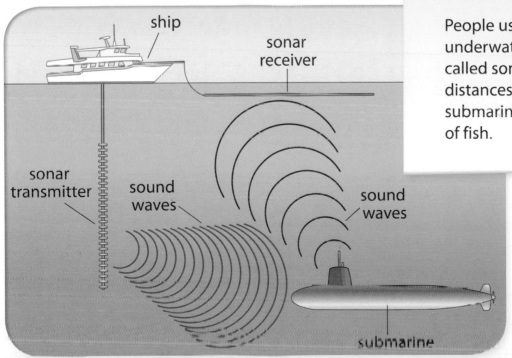

ship

sonar receiver

sonar transmitter

sound waves

sound waves

submarine

Working with bats

Humans have learned a lot from studying bats and finding out more about their special abilities. As well as trying to use technology to copy amazing bat skills, people work with bats in different ways.

Amazing bat poo!

Bat poo is called guano. If you go inside a cave that is home to a colony of bats, one of the first things you will notice is the smell! Guano has very high levels of chemicals in it that make great **fertilizer**. In some places, guano is removed from cave floors and scattered onto fields to help crops grow. People have also used guano to make explosives and cleaning products.

Large amounts of guano can be found in caves where bats roost.

Vampire medicine

Scientists are investigating a substance in vampire bats' **saliva** to see if it can be used to help doctors treat patients. Hospitals might be able to use the substance to help people who have suffered from a **stroke**.

Could vampire bats help doctors save lives?

MEGA POLLINATORS

Megabats are important in forests because they **pollinate** flowers and spread seeds. The bats' feeding activity helps new plants to grow. Many things we use every day, including foods, medicines, clothing, and chewing gum, come from plants that bats pollinate in this way.

The amazing bat

Bats are incredible creatures with a stunning range of skills and senses. Humans need bats to keep many plants growing and to limit the number of insect pests. Sadly, around 25 per cent of the world's bats are threatened with extinction, mainly because humans are destroying their habitats. We need to appreciate what these amazing animals do for us and work to protect them.

Scientists think that this horseshoe bat's unusual nose helps it to use echolocation.

Bat superpowers

If you could choose one of the skills and abilities that bats have, what would you pick? You're already very good at communicating with your species and looking after your friends. But what if you had some bat skills, too?

- If you could fly around, you'd never be late for school again.

- If you could use echolocation to find your way in the dark, you wouldn't need to turn on any lights to find your way to a midnight snack!

- If you could hang upside down, even when you were asleep, that would definitely impress your friends.

- If you could hibernate in the winter, you would have no more cold, dark mornings – you could just wait till spring and wake up then!

- If you could migrate hundreds of kilometres away to a warmer country, it would be perfect for when you fancy a holiday.

These bats are roosting in trees in Queensland, Australia.

Glossary

adapted developed to suit the environment

ambush make a surprise attack

artificial made by humans

colony (plural: **colonies**) large group of bats

echolocation system of finding prey and avoiding obstacles using sounds and echoes

fertilizer substance added to soil to help crops grow

habitat natural home for an animal or plant

hibernate rest to save energy during winter

hover remain in one place in the air

magnetic able to attract certain substances and show the location of north and south

mammal type of warm-blooded animal that has a backbone, feeds on its mother's milk when young, and has hair on its body

megabat type of bat that eats fruit and flowers and mainly lives in Africa, Asia, and Australasia

microbat type of bat that mostly eats insects and other small animals. Microbats live all over the world.

pollinate take pollen from one flower to another so that new plants can be produced

predator animal that hunts and eats other animals

prey animal that is eaten by other animals

roost hang and rest

saliva fluid in the mouth used to digest food

species particular type of living thing

stroke blockage in a blood vessel in the brain

territory area of land where one animal or group of animals belongs

Find out more

Books

Bats, Elizabeth Carney (National Geographic, 2010)

Bats, Megan Cullis (Usborne, 2009)

Websites

www.bats.org.uk

The Bat Conservation Trust's website is full of information about bats in the United Kingdom and around the world. Find out how to adopt a bat!

www.bbc.co.uk/nature/life/Bat

The BBC Nature website has lots of information about different bats and videos of bats in action.

kids.nationalgeographic.com/kids/animals/creaturefeature/vampire-bat

Find out more about vampire bats on the National Geographic website.

Places to visit

Join your local bat group to get involved in spotting bats in the wild. You might be able to take part in conservation projects to help protect bats. Find out more at www.bats.org.uk/pages/local_bat_groups.html.

Take part in the Indicator Bats Program and help monitor bat populations where you live: www.ibats.org.uk

You might be able to see bats at your local zoo or wildlife park.

Index